Still No Sign of Them

Still No Sign of Them

Poems by

Jeanne Renaud

Red Hen Press

1998

Still No Sign of Them
Copyright © 1998 by Jeanne Renaud

Red Hen Press is a division of Valentine Publishing Group.

Acknowledgments:
"Attaching" by Anna Barszczewska first appeared in the magazine *Georgetown Review.*

Cover photograph by Marlene Joyce Pearson
Book design by Mark E. Cull

First Edition
ISBN 1-888996-08-0
Library of Congress Catalog Card Number: 98-84055

Red Hen Press
Valentine Publishing Group
P.O. Box 902582
Palmdale, California 93590-2582

For Dot and Bob

TABLE OF CONTENTS

The Past

THE TRANSLATIONS

THE MARRIAGE

Still No Sign of Them

The Past

To Menlo Park and Back

She breathes in warm leather
sitting tight behind
on the back of her brother's BSA.
He throttles, she slides,
grabs folds of his jacket.

Her hair cold
dips
into curves
like a pendulum,
a Kettenburg tacking into wind.

Lines melt
pavement flashes
the seat vibrates, tickles
the edges.

They lean into El Camino Real
pass the Park Theater,
Johnny Smoke Shop, where once
colored men cut hair, they ate
black licorice and danced on tables
at Fosters Freeze.

You okay back there?
She slips her arms
under his coat
palms against shirt
fingers touching fingers
and purrs
to a world of vibration.

Course

She sits propped up, eyes glued shut,
catheter full of blood.
Dad moistens her tongue and she screams
"I'll kill every one of you!"

Uncle Denny comes by at noon
ends up eating her lunch
Dad says by the door of her room
"He's already been in the hooch."

Mom says it's best this way
she shouldn't last too long
you know how cranky she is
she'd have never lived in a home.

The pacemaker keeps her heart beating
the morphine hurries it up
Everything is sinking
They decide to turn it off.

Everyone thinks she planned it
about a week ago.
She walked us out behind her house
and gave Dad Pop's old tools.

Looking past the fairway
just beyond her fence
she talked about cremation
in that tiny French accent

"Mix my ashes with Pop's," she said,
"along with the seed and dirt
you keep in that old tin can
in the back of your gold cart
and when you're on the green
in an early morning round robin
put us in a divot
left by a five iron."

Little Lives

I'm sailing north along the China coast
on a huge ocean liner towards Japan
to take the fastest train to the largest city.
100 degrees, calm seas.
I rented a surfboard in Waikiki
where the water was all hot and green
like a bathtub.
At night I lay sweating with no covers on
marking off days on my calendar.

I'm going to Cal Poly to satisfy
some creep at the draft board.
The human race is doing its best
to cause people like me to be unhappy!
Somebody built up a beautiful
country before my eyes
then it became a big plastic joke.
I'm searching for a place
where I'll be satisfied.

We're hitchhiking to Alaska
sleeping in the garage of a house filled
with a bunch of holy rollers, who are
actually are, insane!

Northern California and Oregon,
that big green country I've seen in pictures
so like every time I go to L.A.
it puts me on a bummer
that's impossible to forget,
like I'm on my own now, dig?

My life will be a continuing stream
a series of little lives
living in different big houses
with groups of people who will
just by chance be together—
more people, more ideas and a wider range of brain power.

We clean trails in county parks
a buck twenty-five
but I don't have to cut my hair
and it's all outdoors.

I left for this trip cross-country
with no shoes or a jacket,
found the grooviest leather jacket in Big Sur
bought some boots in Utah.
It was snowing in the Rockies.

We dropped acid in Yellowstone
ran out of gas and hitchhiked to get some.

So few people so few towns
more trees and land just lying there.
People in L.A. so sure they know where it's at
people in the Midwest
inquisitive as little kids or cats.

I get so jazzed when I look at the farms
and think about getting one
and a bunch of people
millions of animals and a barn
and a garden and it snows in winter
and a fireplace.

I'm checking again in this store
where I work. Swear people got stupider
since last time I checked.
On my lunch hour I go to the laundromat
and think about food.

AAH! Everything's a big rush.
My feet are soft and white and my face
all fucked from shaving. To this straight
American world, I am insane,
a madman!

I look in the mirror, embarassed
to look so straight
and I just keep reading these comic books
a guy brought over.

Highway 15, Yucatan Peninsula
Desert and wasteland
but now green everywhere
and the jungle keeps getting thicker.
The people are poor and know about life
and soon I will be poor and we will be closer.
Villages, a groovy river and all kinds of
peasants messing around and cows drinking
and the water so blue
and no cops to hassle you. Mexico City
Magic Mushrooms, beaches, oceans, hurricanes
we didn't stop till Laredo and then
only for milkshakes and hamburgers.

I smoked a lot of grass and now
not too much. Depression is a state
of mind no longer experienced fully but remembered
as a thing of my past life. I've got it down to five
words but it keeps changing—
"Time is life, is change."

We have a neat old house
in a strictly colored district
with a groovy old porch, pillars and the like.
Afternoons we play ball in the tree-lined streets.
The Rockies can be seen in the distance.

Spent a night in Taos
picked up this guy hitching
groovy people, met a chick there,
stoneness, outta sight.

I'm living as my father suggested,
can't understand my mother's logic
"I thought you had grown up but I guess not."
Wish I had my red yogi book and my Bible
nothing else
except a woman.

I left this girl behind in Denver,
another in Atlanta,
tired of cities, scenes, going there and finding
out where everything is happening
people—heads.

I want to become part of a small town
where I do something and people
know me by that.

I'd like to meet a groovy, innocent chick
and turn her on to the world.

Hot and Cold

They gave me three squares
and a roof over my head.
One time Mom rubbed
stuff on my legs—
let me climb on her bed.

They came to the hospital
with stick dolls
when I swallowed a penny—
Mom drove recklessly,
the doctors held me upside down.

They liked my performance
when company was over—
they'd drink and smile
and kiss and stuff
and Dad would feel Mom up.

Dad let me order lobster.
Mom clucked, then pouted.
Dad laughed and joked
and we were on the same side.

When I got caught stealing at 14
he threw all my makeup out the car window
socked me and screamed,
"What should we do with you?"

Mom said something happened
at 18 months—
temper tantrums, not wanting
new shoes,
refusing to step on snow.

Despues de Dormir

When it rains in Beverly Hills
Cafe Pavillion closes up.
Farzhad the waiter calls me
from the parking lot.
I watch him from my bedroom window.

Jacob had eye surgery for nearsightedness,
wants the name of a good nose man,
calls me kinky, feeds me macadamias
until my tongue hurts.
When I move my clothes to the dryer,
I take the phone off the hook.

Kazim says I make his mouth water.
He has a girlfriend
but his heart goes
to his mouth
when he thinks of me.

Dentists are usually small.

Michael had his license revoked
for 60 speeding tickets.

Morry calls five times
in one day, tells me I've lost
the warmth in my voice.

Ralph cancels for New Years.
I go to the Plitt
and stand in line with Jack Nicholson.
Now I have to lie to Susan about my date.

Abdi's cute in the morning—
gets up fast, happy.
He's finding a career.
He feeds me broiled shark
corn
and tomatoes.
He wants Irish Whiskey cake
and me on top.

Carlo says he's romantic
with a bite that's prognathic.
He tells me I'm natural, healthy
and beautiful
and I have a soul.
He takes me to Geoffrey's
for brunch and Champagne.

Saul is interested in my cookie idea.

Jacques comes
over with
candies and
bubble bath.
I think we
might
move in
together.
He says be
kind.
Be kind
always.

I send Leyden for butter
and orange juice.
He comes back
with oysters, French bread,
chocolates.
He works at the La Salsa, goes
sleeping and dreaming with burritos.
Pobrecito cocodrelito

Como los niños chiquitos
despues de dormir.
He writes me a poem:

> The bird of your dream
>   is not a bird
>
> It is your life with wings.

Teevee

I used to slam doors
when I heard noise outside.
7 o'clock, Sixty Minutes—fixed horses
drinking in Iceland

Reading my new Mazda manual while watching
an Elvis movie in Hawaii.
Peter Sellers died today.
Ted Kennedy's voice.
He could help her live; he could *not* help her to
decide for what purpose she wished to go on living.

Other people's lives flashing before my
eyes, I take for my own.
Portillo gave Reagan a white Arabian stallion.
Return of hostages
I want to go to Saudi and sit on the beach
where no one else sits.

The waves were 12 feet today.
Disco-Communism hit the Moscow scene
I'm not the girl of his dreams. I'm not the
girl of anyone's dreams even though I've
led some to believe it.

I hear men say all the time
"if I were a woman, I'd never
work."

How nice when the
world cooperates with your
time of rejoicing.

Women are the keepers of the gate.

The one who pays is the boss.
Money money money money money eating
out of your hands every day. I drive to different
parts of the world with my
indigestion.

Why can't my friend be
instead of the TV?

Nowhere to escape.
No more plans to make.
No more energy to carry you to
these plans.
No more beauty or youth to buy you
time.
No more time.
Options keep decreasing.
No more children. No more degrees.
No more possibilities of marriage proposals.
No more money for college.
No job offers when you finally get out.
No chances to travel to faraway places
in hopes of finding a man.
The bloom is gone from your face,
your skin is sallow and dry.
Your is gray and thin.
You are white splotches on your skin.

Reading my Mazda manual
thinking about eating Buhdda-head food
and not saying one trite thing
all evening.
Lambada.

Now you're talking.
No this isn't going the way she
wanted it to go.
She tried to blame the dinner's
failure on them cause she
halfway believed it was all their fault.

Even though he's my boyfriend I
occasionally go out with other people
like my landlord, the guy who bought
my last car, well you get the idea.

The gift that says you'd marry her
all over again

On my 30th birthday Abdi took me to Le Club.
Got some birthday $ from M & D. Mom still
doesn't know what my name is.

I'm waiting for 12:00
so I can eat. I feel
weird eating eggplant
parmesan before that.

I'm watching *The Jerk*, this guy all
of a sudden gets a whole bunch of money.

I broke up with Abdi last night.
He asked me if I wanted to know
what really bothered him about me.
The Women's Room. Orgasm of their life.
She talks! Ingrid Bergman's daughter,
Isabella Rosselini in her Lancôme
commercial.

The capitol building was bombed today.

Abdi's not ready for me—maybe next year.

My tongue is killing me.

Seasonal affective disorder brings about
winter depression.

Jessica Savitch died in an auto accident.

Feeling like a regular in Beverly Hills. It's like
you think that's where it's at but you find
out everybody's there to be where it's at.

I hate driving to work mostly.
Mostly I hate driving to work.

I'm perfect,
beautiful, sexy, wonderful, affectionate, giving, caring
healthy, and I'll give you beautiful children
and make a lovely home for you.

I sort of have a boyfriend.

The sun and wind felt good and I came home.

Teddy Pendergrass.
He's had it with cheap sex. It leaves him feeling
cheap.

Farmers create a shortage by spilling milk to force prices
up.

Went to Ah Fongs for Chinese and caught the Olympic parade
Richard Burton died today.
Peter Jenning looks like someone I know.
Boom boom against bang bang
Bang!
Bang it back
banking them out
growing my bangs out

I want to bang you, baby.
The space spacy age is really here.
Didn't want to spend the night
but asked me to a Dodger's game.

I keep flipping the pillow over.
Men want to talk at night,
women in the morning and afternoon
are needy.
Paul Newman marinara sauce
seek pleasure in nothing
seek to know nothing
seek to possess nothing
seek to be nothing

I need a family.

"I thought you'd be dressed up."
Oh boy I've got to concentrate my efforts now.

I just need time alone in the morning.

Maybe I should do.
Maybe your baby done made some other plans.
Stopped by the Beverly Wilshire for a Sunday *Times*
but they were out.
I'm gonna have to cancel for tonight. I'll get back to
you.
Dean Martin at Carmine's.
Gravitating between things, never
stopping to rest.

He's too, too and to.

He came over and prayed for me.

Mom called. She sounded weird like someone
had died or something.
She had been planning Ellen's wedding for years.

At Le Dome, Olivia Newton John with her new
husband. Gov. Brown with new girlfriend

Ellen's wedding that never was.
Instead I took her
to the merry-go-round
at Griffith Park

And she took off all her Lingerie
Bra and camisole. La Famiglia
End-of-the-season Cliff-hangers

Life is less pleasure than being with you.

Mira and Val. You were the real victims.
Ah Chris. Poor Chris. She never even had a
chance. But for that one year they were all really
happy.

I was always trying.

I actually loved his need
to be told he's good and smart and
wonderful.

Three's Company's on in ten minutes.

Peaches

Half-yawning because of a cold sore
walking up those stairs
in leather lace-up boots,
each man passing my failure.
(It hasn't always been like this)
The men sit on one side of the room
the women the other.
I call my women friends
too ugly to go out in public.

I'm eating with my mouth open,
talking while I'm eating,
choking until
I'm forced to stop,
unable to answer why
I came here.

I blot the wound with my napkin,
reapply my lipstick
careful to go around.

There's a can of cling peaches on the counter.
Peaches won't do it.
If Uncle Vanya doesn't
I'll go to Shipley's for a chocolate
eclair and stay up all night drinking coffee
and reading Frank O'Hara
who got hit by a dune buggy
on Fire Island. It isn't good.
It isn't good. It's nothing.
Only beauty turns my head.

Paris Waiting

60 F for taxi fare
Hotel Agial on the south side
my window with the sun
pizza with egg on top
Castel very very crowded
and smoke we ate at Picolo
everyone knew Francois
beef on toast in pink sauce
fois gras salad to start
orange juice and Perrier for my sore throat
I came out and he was ready in bed and said
I'll just sleep with you
he kissed me told me to call him
and if I needed a doctor he'd send one
omelet with cheese and ham and bread always
laundry detergent such delusions
everything's drying nicely
we drove around Champs Elysees
cars parked down the center (I thought it was an accident)
the Seine Arc de triomphe
Napoleon Bonaparte statues
carvings cars
Place de la Concorde, min. de la defense
I wrote it all down and started out
shops opening
the market
a croissant café au lait
and the Eiffel Tower where John asked directions
we crossed the Seine
St. Augustine
worked out at Monceau
the Rue de Chazelles Le Louvre tomorrow
another dreary day
cold and clouds
and now sprinkles fall weak
with crap in my head along the Vaugrard
to St. Michel to St. Germain the Seine
and it was beautiful

and I could see the Eiffel Tower
and it was stunning
Paris beautiful
their attitude
autos stinky buses honking horns constantly
the Metro
it's Wednesday and tomorrow's Thursday
Je ne parle pas Français
Je ne parle pas Français
he drove pointing everything by night and said
I was wrong that he loved me
sleep good and a big kiss for you
I went downstairs and asked Madame
for an extra pillow
these huge buses they come
they all get in and it takes them away
Cherche Midi (Francois says "stomash" for "stomach")
Rue du four Dragon
where we met Jean-Pierre that first night
like winter claustrophobic and Tim smelling of anchovies
watching me eat ice cream the shape of a penis
leave one bag here
take three to Avignon
12 F for cereal box
7 for pastry 5-7 for café au lait
I'm gonna pay this with my Visa and skeedaddle out of town

Hunter

He's cramping real bad from eating
ground venison
kept too long in the fridge
shot with a compound bow,
a pod of Anictine screwed
into the arrow.

It's a bull's eye to the neck!
cardiac arrest,
respiratory failure,

all the muscles stop.

"Changes him
into a different state,"
he said. "He's hit, shot,
don't have to track him
cause he don't drop."

At the hospital it's
muscle relaxers, an antinausea,
two cc's in the butt.

What I'm Told

The mechanic works
on my carburetor
with parts from his.
I stand watching
behind the screen door.

We drive for U-joints,
he asks why I never go out.
Been out all last week.
Look in my eyes and say it.

I think about the boy who wants me.

I talk of foreign cities, changing
my name.
He reaches under the seat, hands me
unwound videos to return—
In the Buff, Hot Farm Girls
Who Want It.
He looks at me at the light, says
"Do something with that hair."

He tells me he's a famous mechanic.
He's doing the work for free.

Patchouli Oil

The American flag
on the loop of his jeans
sparkles in the sunlight.

She smells Patchouli
dabbed
on a fresh laundered shirt.

Curly dark hair
tied in back
round his heart-shaped face
heart-shaped lips.

Patchouli-oil boy
with wire-rim glasses
she barely noticed
maybe just imagined.
An anchronism

born
when she was going through it.

In shoes from Vermont
he promises her
his heart-shaped vial.

She wants to know him
see if she's changed all that much.

Temp

I never buy furniture,
hang pictures.
I'm going abroad.

I don't have a car
or a job.
I can get them there.

I need new clothes,
a summer wardrobe,
but the climate might be cold.

If they have no apartments
or guest rooms in churches
I wouldn't mind a hotel.

I'll need a new boyfriend.
The old one says, Thailand?
I'm not going to follow you there.

Family Life

". . .my sliver of sky is silvery with it yet . . ."
　　　　　　　　　　—*Samuel Beckett*

It's 1:30 p.m. and me and my neighbor
just woke up. His radio is going.
I'm coloring my hair on those spots,
plastic cap tied on top
like my mother in the rain.

I'm tired of telling him to turn it down.
He doesn't realize
　　the state I'm in.
I'll look in the paper,
sell my computer
my bike
my bed
my couch.
That's all.
Then I'll be free
to fail on my own terms.

When I bang on the wall
my heart races
until he turns it down.
He usually turns it off
and leaves.
Today he turned it off
with no malice or rancor.
He went back to banging his girlfriend,
a young Pat Benatar.

My hair looks great.
Is that music I hear?

Soldiers

Wine stains on Joni Mitchell's face
whose glasses left impressions
she can't see anymore
or remember (no one really remembers
or wants to)
like the Vietnam Vet
who can't let go.
What will he be if he isn't a soldier?
What will she be if she isn't a flower child?

She's prettier now:
she fixed her teeth.

Glad when everyone has forgotten the sixties,
waiting to forget today.

lose weight
cut your hair
stop drinking and smoking dope.

Your life is under control.

Getting Help

He speaks softly
sits across from you.
Space. Personal.
Plenty of that.
His head cocked
like a gun
waiting.
He does it
so you'll look. Always
looking into the eyes,
one to the other until
you're blear-eyed,
hard of hearing.

He sips from a Coke can
that sounds empty.
"What do you want to work on here?"
He makes you relax
in his Imperial chair.

Evening on New Year's Dream

These people next door with their music
real loud. I'd move
but I only got four months
and there's the phone
and finding someone with a truck
and my back.
How sweet it will be
in the morning, them
with their sore throats
and headaches, me
sleeping soundly to the hum
of my refrigerator,
dreaming of a swallow
perched unsteadily on my finger.
I want to keep him
alive, force worms
down his throat
but my father tells me
It's impossible it won't work.
Still I let him wobble to and fro,
feel his tiny claws.

When the refrigerator kicks off
I hear the wailing sound—
the kind of music
that used to put me to sleep.

If I close my eyes I can continue
my dream.

Patient For You

You're sitting on
an island in the air
with David Letterman below
behind his big desk,
laughing

He gestures his head
to his new white shoes,
tight and stiff,
with uneven heel counters.

"What's the answer to question
#2?" he asks.

It takes too long to say it
but Letterman is patient,
he's laughing.

If you answer correctly you
get to shoot him with a
squeegy-ball gun.

It takes three times to hit him,
Letterman is patient.

It bounces off something
attached to his tie.

Prayer For My Daughter

I was only three years younger than you are now
cocksure and stupid. I'm sorry
I wasn't there.
But having a father is no big deal.
You would've ended up hating me.
I would have pushed and pleaded
even though I meant not to.
This way you have only fond thoughts.
You put me on a pedestal.
It's my loss.
But I really cannot know
how you feel.
I've never been a daughter
without a father.
I hope it gets better as you get older.

Fortune

Stop the joke and send me back.
I can't hide it, though I try.
Color the gray hair
but it keeps coming back fuller, short leg
keeps getting shorter.
Exercise the flabby skin
but it keeps getting looser.
Bleach the teeth white though it costs a fortune.
Grow my hair long to hide the folds
when I turn my head.
And what about the things you can't see
like the teeny bladder
the bad back
the creaking bones
bad eyesight.

Married

He sits on the neighbor's
Airgometer, feet
wavering between
pedal and footrest,

reading history
on the distance-traveled monitor.
Listen to that four-barrel.
He's taking her for a spin.
He puts on the ear clip,
plugs in the cord,
then watches his pulse go up.

She thinks about the wife and him
that day from the picture window—
his bounce
her hair—
how they both wore glasses.

He hears the spring of a screen
door stretch like a yawn
dismounts
swinging his leg around.

The neighbor smiles and
waves bye
while the wife, between their doors
sees the crossed legs,
the bicycle shorts.

As they disappear behind their door,
the neighbor sees the bicycle wheel spinning,
hears the wife's
"What the hell are you doing?"

Haircut

"Hope springs eternal." Some line
from some poem somewhere.

Anyway, how is it with you?
Does the new haircut drive
your freshman boys wild?
They may be inexperienced
but they've got so much *energy*
(or at least I remember it
that way). There's this one

who sends me little "love" notes
always quite subtle
and shy but the young yearning there
in all its glory.

"Ahh . . . Spring . . ."
Soon lovers will begin spilling
across grassy fields.
Let's join them. Let's
fall in love
at least for one more season.

Adulterated Emotions

After she got on board
I hung around her plane
listening to Frankie S.

I sat on the rim
of the big picture window.
Her plane pulled away from the gate.
(seemed like it was there a long time)

I got up and waved
followed it to the next set of windows
still waving.
You've seen people like this at airports
Waving
for all that it's worth.

I traced through the terminal.
A big hollow inside
wondering if my emotions were genuine
or adulterated by my desire

to witness
to record
to document the moment.

The Berry Gatherers

He says I'll never let you go
but I'm still looking for an escape route.
He says you need someone like your father
who bitches at you.

Words are cheap but
feelings know.

The berry gatherers are tired of
lying to themselves.
Lerner lost $5 million
in the stock market this year.
Dad sent a hundred dollars,
said he'll send more when he gets rich.

I don't know what death smells like
ice cream and lightbulbs?
Last week it was 18°
tomorrow's supposed to be 80.

I called Ellen. Said
she lost thirty pounds.
She sounded skinnier.
I fell asleep and dreamed
of being in the Turkish Army.
Go forward young men

He said he'd always be there
but got uncomfortable when I felt him
relieving me of my duties.

"Don't I get at least one crack back?
Fuck you, you fucking ballbuster"

I'm entering a new phase in my life
not to be taken seriously
but rather to be enjoyed,
a creative phase a happy phase,
a loving, warm and mystical phase,
fluffy from now on
and we'll look ahead to the future
with joy and renewed excitement.

My hairdresser goes, "ya know Didi
from Hunter?"
He fabricated this idea that
I'm breaking up with him
because I criticized
his treatment of the door-to-door salesman,
ejected from normal life.
It never did make sense,
it never did to me.
He didn't get what he thought he was getting.

peu à peu
l'oiseau fait son nid.

It's getting later
the weather's getting cold.

I want someone to cook.

What I Want

We still say I love you,
he still calls me honey,
I'm still in his prayers every night.

He's going to that wide open
country, where he can see
the Braves if he likes. The

kind of place he knows I'd
like, that we often spoke of
trying. He says "It's been

hard here lately but I've
finally learned to let go.
If you see me around

don't think I'm cold." He's
been out with others, plenty
of offers, but something in

their eyes makes him pull
back. Do you want to write,
I ask. No problem in that,

he says. He wishes only
the best for me. He hopes
I get what I want.

One Day

idea from an untitled poem by Tomas Salamun

one day I woke from a good night's sleep
a nice dress
had eaten all the right things
the right amounts
one day I ate the sweetest orange and thought
the littlest ones are usually the best
one day I pulled my fingers through my hair
until no more hairs appeared between them
one day it was a bad day and I saw everyone
though I tried not to
one day it was a good day and I saw no one
so I drove to DC
but when I got there
it wasn't the same day
one day the people next door moved away
one day I didn't care anymore
and he came back
one day I found myself in between
one day I saw Sbardella in the paper
holding up a sign that said

    This   Helicopter
     is   Loud
    It is disturbing
      The   Peace

and called to tell him
but hung up
one day I might not stop doing things like this

Brown

At sixteen he went
Sailing . . .
but that's another story.
How many more times when I
hear "Brown-eyed Girl" will
I be sixteen, sunk
in the back seat of Frank
Cosetti's Yellow Firebird
(he drove it all the way to Alaska
and back without sleep)
sailing
along Palos Verdes Drive North
smoking a jay, feet up
on the plush, suntan
lotion and sand
in my hair, the ocean
to my left, thinking
My eyes aren't brown.

Out of Habit

Waiting on the couch,
feet on the coffee table,
papers in my hand
and the sound turned down.
I'm thinking
about how your mouth
moves when you talk
on the phone, breathing
in the spaces, teeth
tugging your lower lip,
tongue appearing in a smile.
And how, at the kitchen table
legs crossed long, mouth
going wide to close
around the filter, you pull
long on your cigarette
out of habit.
With wide eyes
your teeth mash, crush
the filter
till it's wet.

Jack

a door slamming
shakes me from my dream
cars coming going
thump thump thump
from the room next door
there's a party going on
he knows about
my bed
it wasn't the beginning
of anything
I had a nice one he said
his voice the sweet music
of a man
our mouths raged
the floury smell of his shirt

it's almost gone now
cars coming and going
never see him
only hear his side
thump thump
and him trying to put his hand there
and me trying to say no
to make it last

Close

He has that grown-up smell
of coffee and cigarettes.

We decide to leave
together. In separate
wooden chairs we share
a cigarette.

I lie back on the porch stoop
in my Grape Taffeta
our eyes to the stars.

He steps into my rocket
and we kiss
until my arm falls asleep.

The soft indent of my thigh
reminds him of
someone.

We let the dogs in and
he tells me the story about joining the Marines.

The Translations

Beggarwoman

by Ann Barszczewska

Defend
the immunity of a woman's wrinkles
stooped
over cupped palm
when the roar of the city unseen
goes by

Only the pavement's point of view
reveals the crevice
through which the world shows
its naked heels

Defend it
maybe in the lips' grimace
you can find a paradox
fed
with air and freedom of sight

Afterwards

by Anna Barszczewska

The world went out
one morning
Now it is stealing
approaching
always the same way
with hopes of my death
by chronic solitude
only common trials
of painless respiration
      (still unsuccessful)
and words written by me
for which I beg your pardon
connect us
those far and even farther
who are equally strangers

by Anna Barszczewska

Words which are grown in the body
protect
but still I tear them out
I give them up to the whiteness of the paper
by voluntarily sentencing them to memory

so that I may sometime
catch a letter
and draw myself in
with the strength of my muscles
there
where there's still the taste of air
where pain has honor

by Anna Barszczewska

They flow
two messengers of existence

They flow
they bore new elements of a face
in an unfinished picture

They flow
undeniable
incomprehensible
washing out the dark traces of the brushstroke's
strange eyes and hands

They fall shivering
singular
absurd
rainfalls of life and death

by Anna Barszczewska

Then
when no one believes
you devote yourself
and all the rest
to a word
and it can't be otherwise
silence becomes a blessing
a short groan of astonishment
is a sin
I wait for the intended
stone

Attaching

by Anna Barszczewska

I love air the most
its indifferent coolness cleansing my skin
coolness
which comes in and leaves
without pain

People and things are scattered by my hand
sometimes I touch their faces
the cold face of a lantern
the warm face of my mother
whom I left one day as everyone does
without remorse
the urgent face of my husband
leaving me always
on the other side of his body
Sometimes I touch . . .
but carefully always carefully

I love air the most
I didn't try to keep it longer and longer
this love without condition
each of us can leave
without loneliness or despair
only
tree branches hanging somewhere high
where wind every now and then changes direction

Falling Down

by Adam Mierzwinski

Golden tulip tree leaf
Began the autumn season
Autumn crunchy, mild
That's you
Who was going out to meet me
through notes you left for me
I could feel you close by
when I came from work
Hard work in the coal mine
White swan on the smooth lake
is proud
and won't come to us

The bakery shop is the lowest place
so you can choose whatever you want
Now it is closed
They said out of business
No! It is no movie
I have to wake up
To the next autumn day
Next fight

The Marriage

Iwona's House

Babcia's pounding meat upstairs
The TV's just been turned down.
This is Novy Sacz, Iwona's house
And Iwona's out doing the hula hoop
Among the dahlias and hyacinths.

June and 75°
Colder inside than out
After the rain you can smell
The chickens. We'll eat
Their eggs for dinner tonight.
Tick Tock Tick Tock
The cuckoo clock strikes seven
And the toilet goes off like a cannon.

Grochowka

I.

I love you in bed
I love your smiling eyes
I love you laughing
I love you watching TV
I love you hanging on me
I love you sitting across from me at the table
Your legs are crossed like the trunks
of my young ficus
I love you making breakfast for yourself
I love you coming home from work
I love you walking through the house
your walk, your steps
I love you at sunrise time
I love you eating grochowka
I love you cleaning the toilet
I love you chewing my pink bubble gum
the scent of your hair
when you keep your legs on me
like you are all mine

II.

I love to hear my stomach move with your breath
the resonance of your heart
You are not a doll
I am King for a night and a day with no duties
out of service

I love the passing of time without my guard
with no resistance from you

I sometimes even love your complaining
about stupid things

I love it
You are my sweet river

Falling

I sleep in a room in your house
You visit me often
I am man, man should pay
We will be straight with each other
Sometimes can happen
You will be like my sister
Everything I have is yours
I like your eyes
Would you like to go for ice cream?
You can use my car
What about that?
Poor Jeanne
Let me kiss it

I have a room in your house
I listen for movement on the other side
a deep voice that is yours
Sometimes you yell at your children
Your car is parked in your new parking garage
I have trouble looking at you
I envy your daughter who sleeps with you
and your son who looks up to you
and tries so hard to please you

Higher

I come to lie upon a higher place
a brighter room
with wooden floors
and velvet curtains

on a healing pad
for the old and disabled

but I am not old
He has left me in a book to become
young again

I look beautiful
in the reflection
of the TV
(I am beautiful)

His hands work
the remote control, peel
skin off potatoes,
carry me off

Adam

With the door closed tight, Tom Petty
up, can't hear a thing
on your side—
high pitch of the ringing phone,
cupboards banging,
the knock on my door.
The voice on the other side
is not a voice
but vibration
made by a mouth.
I listen for songs to record,
buy you French cologne.
You walk a few steps behind.

Blasphemy

I wish I could get drunk
or take some kind of pill
get back on track
straighten my stockings
(that was my line anyway)
Don't look at me honey

In need of Mexican food
anything fast food
Chinese take-out
At the "Chinese Restaurant"
they serve meatballs with rice
and throw a bottle of soy sauce on the table
Frozen Pirogi
at the Central Sam
on Jagiellonska
Cheap red wine from Argentina
for Iwona

Only two glasses and already
the guilt of taking up the living room
Can't stand the smell of it
the thought
the thought of waiting forever

Winner

They're building another apartment
upstairs, a third floor.
Hammers are constant from 7 o'clock on.
I get out of bed ache in my head.
It will be dull—an upside
down cake with no brown sugar.
I'm trying to win you
trying to say all the right things,
but you have your children
and the wife who died.

I can turn ugly
I can shout, "No, you're wasting my time
with your words" and you'll stop
and say "Excuse me" with your soft voice,
walk out of the room
leaving me.
I'll show you, I'll
teach you good.

Forgot

I stumbled upon your
graduation pictures today
tucked deep inside
the Norton Anthology
of World Masterpieces
(the only thing left in English to read)
Fifth Edition with self-
portrait of Van Gogh on
the cover with the ear
that's still intact but awfully
pinky red.
I cried.

You're smiling that winning
smile trying to look
like a normal tall guy
in a suit
on graduation day.

You sent me a postcard
of "A Stormy Night:"
where you wrote,

He did it for you
He did it for me
He did it for all of us.

Cold

Cold in this house,
empty clock ticking to the tune

of my headache. Sounds of children,
civilization outside

where it's warm.
He should be pulling up anytime

with his golden-haired corka.
I fill my days with dinners.

I could maybe get a flat
and we could work out the work.

He's trying to get in,
fiddling with keys in the door.

Mississippi

So hot that when you lie down
your chin sticks
to your shoulder.
I bought a whopping
$3.00 *Vogue* with Kim
Basinger on the cover who I
felt kin to cause two boyfriends
now "friends" told me I looked
like her. I never saw the
resemblance except maybe the
deep-set eyes and blonde hair.
Tin roof ice cream, Spanish
peanuts, bread and cheese, apple
and a *TV Guide*.

Sitting on a borrowed beanbag chair
switching back and forth from
TV Guide to *Vogue*.
Blue-Bell ice cream. Seems
our store started getting
it when they heard it was Bush's
favorite. I started buying it
cause it was the only decent brand
they stocked in smaller
than half-pound cartons.

Dad's visit to H'burg—
seeing zoo (Bear etc.)
Giving gold watch to Mom and her
promise to give me.

I lift my shirt and find peanut skins
stuck to my skin.

I get up to wash my feet again.

Immigration Marriage

We got married today
by the Justice of the Peace
at the municipal building
in McKean, Pennsylvania.

The woman before us—
her son caught with
possession.

They walked in and out of rooms
while we waited
on church pews.

We stood alone in a room
with the smell of sleeping people
with a man who read us our vows
and made us recite.

My foreign husband
didn't always understand
but we left with rings on our fingers
and a kiss that was too loud
and too quick.

Sunday Night

Sunday night when a good pen
is so essential.
When you're so afraid you'll
stop loving him
and start the long road
down.

When your job is on the line
there's a chance you won't
get paid and
no one's to blame.

When it's 13 below
and you've forgotten how to make it
Celsius.

When they've come home from church
and they want to play cards
and he asks you for things
and you have to remind him
of essentials.

Bluegreen

The TV is what the fireplace used to be
supposed to used to
light yellow refrigerator
writing for the urgent soft sound of
your Nikes
the neighbor with his girlfriend who laughs
uncontrollably
through walls
like sky that nestles between those hills
with fences

The sky is blue and the earth is brown
green so green it's blue

We floated down the Dunajec
You bathed in my bathwater
joined me in fitting rooms

Dreams

Living apart has its advantages.
Sometimes I think it would be easier to be mad,
a house in the country.

Snuggly pups silky, a filly,
furniture
a house you can look at, touch, smell,
ride.
What about doing what he wants—
I could have all that.

Sitting half in, half out
of a sun that carries a warm breeze
slippers on blue concrete of a balcony
inside carpet, white, the window—
a portrait of leaves and branches
a single yellow rose in a crystal vase
(pronounced vahz)
from a marriage where we lived
together and then
apart, where it wasn't enough
to hold it together.
I get these roses often.
I fear for my life.

A couple empty boxes in the corner
books against the wall
and the kitchen nook you always
wanted, typewriter on the floor.

A feeling of being ill and never
getting better
of being a pupless couple
with no room to ride
no space to fill.

Mom's bringing lasagne,
we've got the grill
and Paul Newman's dressing.
It will be festive, with blue
for landscape, yellow roses, they're
busy cleaning rooms.

Brand new socks faded red,
old brick building
and the buttercups of yellow
to give it a chance.

Change for the laundry
where the blue slowly fades
where time sits still
and we are meant to see
the metallic green insects
hovering about the screen door
coming awfully close.

Lawnmower

It's Sunday almost gone.
You live in a house man and wife.
He sleeps in the other room
speaks his language

It's been there for a while but you
all of a sudden
realize the neighborhood noise
of a lawnmower (he calls it mover)
is your husband
but he is no longer
doing it
for the feeling he's giving you.

He's keeping busy and carrying on
preparing for the spring garden
for when you will no longer hear
his daughter's laughter as he sits
in a chair
in the corner of her room
with the door not closed
but touching.

When somebody's lawnmower
will just be somebody's lawnmower.

I go to the kitchen window and watch
him for awhile.
He looks up and I wave.

I eat some of his ripe strawberries
and feel like a thief.

Colicy Virus

It begins
foaming at the mouth
She lies on your chest, heavy
like a lover about to jump
You sniff each other

They read her temperature
shoot liquid under the skin
for dehydration

Her teeth snap
like an alligator's
and the pill winds up on the floor
until there's nothing left
but bloody hands
on which you crawl to him

She creeps to the door
teeth chattering, adding
support to the argument
third eyelid opaque
like the skin between
the shell and egg

He bends down to her

Fired

"We're not going to be able to keep you"

you wait for the odor
the words left behind
like a jar of Miracle Whip
that falls from tall expectations
and you land inside
where lions
ask you to make it easy for them

you play dead
and tell them you can make more
alive
and they lick you all over
and it feels good

a meteor falls
into your lap into a dozen
artifacts—

a monkey
a bird
a corpse with living toes
marble, wood
a body partly real and partly clothed
you put in a museum

but they slip through and your sister
and step
daughter use them for dolls

Father's inside and won't
help you, said it was your fault
you shouldn't have been there

You flatten yourself against saltwater
bad references,
scream for your mother
who's hysterical
blind
deaf
and in denial

Xmas

I'm sitting
no I'm caught
cut
caught

he can't hear the difference
until he says the Polish
word for cat: côt
why can't I bring
my kitty for xmas well
I guess so I mean
I don't know
is it an outside cat?
Lucy with the changing
eyes like mine
she puts herself strongly
against me
for sleeping
I want to paint her nose

why must I
why must I think
why is everyone trying
what's the matter with
everyone?

one is gray with blue eyes
I want that one
but they give me Lucy
and we are we
now I'm afraid
I don't want to comb my hair anymore

she's too big for
her kitty condo
but she sleeps there
a small circle of velvet
her tail wrapped inside
one leg dangling over the edge

the heater clicks off
crunch crunch
her blue plastic bowl
she runs around the house like a madman

the toilet seat is cold
I hurt to go out
she likes to get close
I worry
I worry what will happen
if I stop

Black

I left a message on his phone
if I wanted to
I could change
if I could
I wouldn't
I don't dare go
to a movie
too close for
up close and
my hands shake
my head hurts
my hands are red
my pen is black
my loveseat is dirty (I eat my dinner there)
my nightgown says
Beach
and is the color

Losing Not Having

I've made her into a dog
she comes when called,
sits on my chest and licks
my face
drinks from my bathwater
follows me everywhere
Maybe it's just a day for sitting
I'm writing lines on my word processor
I don't dare call anyone
make any plans
I can't make the waiting
into something else

I don't dare watch TV
I don't dare go walking
or shopping
I don't dare eat or sleep

She leaves the wet of her nose
on my chin somewhere

You

I don't need much

a tree, grass,
solitude

a place up high, the sun,
a view

words, air,
a place to fall

The Other Woman

When I came home they were gone
I knew where he was

I ate alone
with fists on the table
slammed doors

I looked out the window

Closed the door of her room
so I couldn't see
what he sees
and loves

I left him a note to join me there

I came back

Still no sign of them

Day After

A bad taste in my mouth
A lot of mucus
always that dull headache
Sun beating on my back
the silhouette of hair across the page

String of apples from the neighbor's tree
on my, our, his side
of the fence
Rumble tunnel of train
of plane overhead
like a lot of traffic

The occasional bark of the dog

I held him while he slept, touched
his face, his mouth
his nice bum, the perfect soft
ones

He sat up the way he always does
First looking at the clock
First putting his glasses on

I held on tight

Detaching

When you stop being a part of it
you notice him starting to tell
his kids to do stuff.
You hear him say, It
doesn't have anything to do with her.
His English is better,
he calls you "her."
He's being polite
letting you down
so you can turn around.

Grover Beach

Screech of tire
loud engines
like buzzing fly
ugliness

There are cars parked on this
beach
Some watch the ocean
the endless tubes of tinfoil

others sleep and enjoy the sun

The hills are a box
with serrated edge

I'm on the edge
of the ice plant
with their stern purple flowers
shimmer of white
not brilliance like the sea
They could be cactii
like that commercial

A small plane in the air
The couple who watch me
and are glad

A white-haired man driving
with his car door open,
walking his dog

A car passing three
horsemen

The kite string I walk
under and think
ladder

The foam left by the sea
I take for a sand dollar
and try to pick up

The runner and his fire
engine dog who won't
stop for anything

The Aquamarine
of the Pismo Pier

The little white dog, always old
and disoriented

The couple who gather
for home

A man connected to earth by a leash

Biographical Note

Jeanne Renaud has an M.S. in Exercise Physiology and a Ph.D. in English from the University of Southern Mississippi. She has published poetry in *Northwest Review* and *Georgetown Review*.